EXPERIENCES AND INSIGHTS

A Journey with God

By

Frank Esposito Jr.

ESPOBOOKS INC.

A Book of Experiences and Insights

A Journey with God

Copyright © 2018 by Frank Esposito Jr.

Frank Esposito Jr.
P.O. Box 66913
St. Pete Beach, FL 33736

Published in 2018 by ESPOBOOKS, INC.

ISBN: 978-0-9906458-4-9

Library of Congress Control Number: 2018905123

Jacket Design by www.scottross.com

Dedication

This book is dedicated with love to Ethan, Julianna, Tyler, Rory, Arden, and Ansley.

Acknowledgements

I want to thank my wife, Marilyn, who contributed her skills and offered support throughout this project. To Carol Marquardt, Fr. Jean Robitaille, M. Afr., and Don Morris for reviewing this book and for their suggestions. To Scott Ross, who designed the book cover. To Nick Harper for his friendship and encouragement. To Ruth Liss for her editorial contributions. And to my prayer group in St. Petersburg, FL who faithfully prayed for me and the book.

TABLE OF CONTENTS

Experiences and Insights

A Journey with God

INTRODUCTION

INTRODUCTION

There are several things that are constant as we journey through life. Day to day, week to week, year after year, events take place that will impact our lives and bring about change in us.

All of us share the same human condition. We have similar (maybe even the same) pressures and struggles in our lives. Sometimes the way we deal with them creates more problems for us. There have been times when I have felt broken and defeated (I think most of us have been there). In the following pages, several of my life experiences will serve as a vehicle to point out some of the ways our lives can get out of order. Some of the examples I share are simple, basic. Yet, they contain valuable lessons. Along with them, I also

1

include suggestions to help us overcome our problems.

Another constant is that God is present with us at all times. Each one of us is created in His image and receives His love throughout our lives, whether we acknowledge Him or not. No matter how far we fall, nor how big a mess we make of things, God will help us if we choose to seek Him and trust Him.

This book is not only about learning from my mistakes. It also contains lessons I learned from observing and listening to others. However, this book is not about me or anyone else for that matter. This book is really about God.

It is my hope and prayer that you will see God's care and faithfulness throughout.

May it deepen your faith, bring you hope and help you experience His love.

AN IMPORTANT LESSON

Chapter 1

An Important Lesson

One of the most valuable things we can benefit from is to learn from our mistakes. Every mistake we make can serve as a teacher to improve our lives if we are willing to learn the lesson each mistake holds. Sometimes we can be slow learners. It took me a while to realize this when it came to how I dealt with God.

You see, for much of my life, whenever I faced a big problem I would pray in earnest and would take everything God had to offer. Most often, I would experience a reassurance that He was with me. That He cared for me. And that He was helping me resolve my problem. I was a taker not a giver. I would not give God what He desired from me. Although, His still, small voice would encourage me to draw closer to Him, follow Him and trust Him.

I believe most of us have been there, done that. A big problem hits our life and we worry or get scared (or both). We spill our heart out to God, asking for His help. Then, when He answers our prayers, we go back to the same lifestyle we led before. Lord, thank you very much for all your help. But, I don't need You anymore. That is, until the next time. Over the course of time, I found myself relying on God's love and kindness to get what I wanted during tough times only to return to my old ways once it was over. This scenario repeated itself many times over.

Eventually, I began to realize some things. Through each problem or trial, God was only a short whispered prayer away. He was always available, reaching out for me regardless of my situation. I say this with total conviction. God never gave up on me, and He will never give up on you if you turn to Him for help.

As I look back at the problems and trials I had (especially when I was younger), I realize that God was constantly trying to get my attention. His desire was that I change course and quit doing things that were contrary to His will and ultimately harmful to me. As I already mentioned, I can be a slow learner.

It was not until I was faced with a serious surgery and the possible amputation of my left leg that for the first time in my life I read the Bible, stopped to really pray, really listen to God, and really decide to be obedient to His will.

You see, all along God had a good plan for me. With the passage of time I learned that the plans He had for me were much better than the plans I had for myself. "For I know well the plans I have in mind for you, says the Lord, plans for your welfare, not for woe! plans to give you a future full of hope." *(Jeremiah 29:11 NAB)* The Lord wants what is best for each of us. With Him there is no favoritism *(Acts 10:34, Romans 2:11, Ephesians 6:9)*. He wants what is best for you too.

So, the first important lesson I want to share with you is that God loves you. No matter what you are going through you are His child and He loves you. Yet, while you are assured of His steadfast love, please avoid the mistake I made of seeking Him only when I had a great need, then pushing Him aside and returning to my old ways once my needs were met.

An Example

Seeking God, then pushing Him off to the side can happen in many ways. Let me illustrate it with one of my experiences.

I attended Palm Beach Junior College and later St. Thomas University on baseball scholarships. I followed an aggressive training regimen which included working out with weights. During my junior year I increased the amount of weights in one of the exercises beyond what was prudent. As a result, I developed a crunching, popping sensation in my left shoulder whenever I lifted my arm. Along with any movement there was a great deal of pain.

My coach referred me to an orthopedic specialist who told me I needed an operation. Undergoing surgery and the necessary rehab meant that I would miss playing my senior year and along with it, end my baseball career. Please understand, my life at that time revolved around baseball, training and pursuing every opportunity to have a good time. I was not a churchgoer, nor was I practicing the faith I was raised with. Nevertheless, I was desperate. My dream to play professional baseball was on the line. I began to pray, begging God to help me. And, He answered my prayer in a way I did not expect.

My mother had dislocated her right shoulder several times. As a result, it was unstable. She made an appointment with one of the leading orthopedic surgeons in the country, and asked me to take her. Unexpectedly, at the end of her consult, she told him about my shoulder problem and asked him to please take a look. He evaluated me and told me to rest my shoulder, follow up with physical therapy, then begin strengthening exercises using light weights. I never had a problem again. So, what did I do? I said, thank you God. Then I resumed playing baseball and returned to my old lifestyle.

At this point, feel free to interject your own similar experience. I think many of us have been guilty of trying to make deals with God in an attempt to manipulate Him. Please remember this, the trials God allows to come our way are designed to teach us and draw us closer to Him. To reiterate what I previously said, God loves you. His perfect, steadfast love will guide you and see you through <u>every</u> trial that comes your way.

THE BEST GPS

Chapter 2

THE BEST GPS

Sometimes we may not even be aware of a mistake we are making because it is unfolding gradually over a long period of time. All of a sudden we may realize that things have changed for the worse in our lives and we ask ourselves what happened? How did I get here?

For example, as a young boy I enjoyed hiking and exploring on my own. At that time, my parents owned a small house near a remote beach. Quite often, as I took long walks along the beach and dunes, I developed the habit of talking to God. I would tell Him all the things I wanted or needed as well as my hopes and dreams. Not only did I speak to God in my own words, I also developed the habit of listening to Him. Even at that young age I intuitively knew God was speaking to me through the thoughts that entered my mind. Talking to God in my own words, praying and listening to Him became ingrained in me as I grew up.

Despite the closeness I felt to God, other influences also entered my life, which competed with Him for my attention as I grew. From the time I began competing I found success in sports. As I grew older I enjoyed the popularity it brought me with my classmates. I liked reading newspaper articles in the sports section that mentioned me. It made me feel good when I was recognized by others in public (especially if

I was with my girlfriend). I also started drinking and going to a lot of parties. Little by little my priorities began to change. I became more concerned with achieving the things I wanted to do and less interested in seeking God for guidance. This did not happen overnight. It was a gradual process spread out over years.

As you can see, I started my journey with God by my side. Then over time I began to lose my way as I continued to push Him aside. Let me illustrate it this way. Many of us when we go on a trip will program our destination with a GPS. The GPS then provides us with the information we need to arrive where we want to go. It tells us to go straight, take a left, take a right, etc. Even if we make a wrong turn and get off course, it will readjust and give us new directions to enable us to arrive at our destination.

In a similar way, God is our GPS. No matter how many wrong turns you make, he will help you make the corrections you need in your life's journey if you ask Him.

LESSONS: GROWING UP

Chapter 3

LESSONS: GROWING UP

In this chapter, I want to share several valuable lessons I learned growing up. Along with them, I will offer some spiritual insights, which I learned over time.

An Algebra Lesson

When I was in the 7th grade, I was
placed in an algebra class with all the
smartest kids in the school. After about one
month, I was not able to keep up and found
myself falling further and further behind.
Frustration, embarrassment and fear took
hold of me.

I turned to my father for guidance as I
struggled with my situation. He spoke with
my teacher, and later all of us had a
conference. By this time I felt I was
hopelessly behind and simply wanted out.
Besides feeling like a failure, my greatest
concern was that I was letting my parents
down, and they would be ashamed of me.

During this time, I had some long
conversations with my father regarding how

hard I was trying and the significance of giving up. But, the most important thing he said to me was that no matter what happened, his love for me would not change. What mattered to him was that I gave my best effort. Ultimately, I transferred to a regular class. However, what I learned through this experience has stayed with me throughout my life.

As much as your father loves you, your Heavenly Father loves you even more perfectly. It is difficult for us to comprehend that He wants to share the same oneness and love with us that Jesus expressed in His prayer. "I in them and you in me, that they may be brought to perfection as one, that the world may know that you sent me, and that you loved them even as you loved me." *(John 17:23 NAB)*

Our Heavenly Father's love for you does not waver or change. He knows every detail about your life. He understands every fault, every shortcoming and is ready to assist you the moment you call out to Him. When you fall flat on your face, He will help you up. Even if perfection is beyond your ability, just give Him your best effort. Give Him all you have. That is enough. That is all He requires.

One other thing, your Heavenly Father does not need your wealth, accomplishments, titles or degrees. He wants your heart. He wants your very best. He wants you just as you are.

A Football Challenge

Most of us come from different backgrounds and have different experiences as we grow up. Whatever interests we pursue in life will provide us with opportunities to learn lessons that we will carry throughout our lives. The following lessons came from my involvement in various sports.

I attended a high school in West Palm Beach, FL that had a rich football tradition. The head coach was successful, demanding and a master psychologist. When I arrived, I quickly realized I had entered into a higher level of competitive sport. Being new to the team I needed to prove myself to my coaches and teammates. I worked hard, played hard and made the first team. One day I arrived for practice and my position coach told me I had been demoted to second team. No reason was given. I was bewildered. Several days later I arrived at practice, and my position coach told me I had been demoted to third team. Why coach? Why was I demoted? He said he did not know; it was not his decision. I was heartbroken. I had given my all to prove myself the best at my position. I was new and now I felt all alone and betrayed. As I processed what had happened, my sadness turned into a new determination to prove them all wrong. The next day and every day thereafter during the one-on-one blocking and tackling drills, I would single out one of the players that had taken my place and do my best to outplay them. I was driven to prove to myself and everyone else that I belonged on the first team.

Another day I arrived for practice and my position coach again took me aside. Frank, you're back on first team. I asked him for an explanation of what had happened to me. He informed me that we had a championship team. The head coach knew all the other starters well and had confidence in them. But, he needed to find out how I would handle adversity. My demotions were tests to see if he could count on me when things got tough.

As you journey through life, you may enter areas that are unfamiliar to you. You may feel alone and isolated as you encounter new situations, new challenges, and new people. Yet, you are never alone. Jesus promised to be with you always *(Matthew 28:20)*. He also said, "I will not leave you orphans; I will come to you." *(John 14:18*

NAB) It is reassuring and comforting to know that He will always faithfully keep His word to you. You can count on Jesus at all times under every circumstance.

Invariably everyone encounters adversity in some form. In this instance, I dealt with demotions that made no sense. You, too, may face a situation you can't explain or understand. You may feel abandoned, all alone. You may be overwhelmed by the situation you are facing. What can you do when you reach this point? What is the best thing to do? Refocus. Turn your eyes away from your problem and turn them to God. Seek His help. Then, use all your energy and strength to pursue His will. Finally, trust Him to keep His word. "We know that all things work for good for those who love God, who are called according to his purpose."

(Romans 8:28 NAB) He has never failed me, and I know with all my heart He will never fail you either.

Perseverance

From an early age I was interested in
martial arts. When I was eight years old my
parents enrolled me in a school of Judo. At
the time I was overweight, weak and
clumsy. I was also intimidated by the way
my Japanese instructors looked and spoke.
However, with the passage of time, I grew to
know them and understand them.

My family moved when I was ten years
old, and I was not able to pursue Judo again
until I was in college in Miami, FL. After
my graduation I moved to Palm Beach
County. At that time, there were no Judo
schools in the area. Therefore, I decided to
study Okinawan Uechi Ryu Karate. I
vividly recall how self-conscious I felt and
how awkward I was when I began my
training. In contrast, my teachers and senior

students were fluid, graceful, and controlled in their blocks, punches, kicks and movements. I recollect thinking it would take me many years to reach their level. I even questioned whether I had the ability to do so.

To make my path even more difficult, the school (DoJo) was almost one hour away from my home. That meant that for years to come, two or three times every week (depending on the class schedule), I would have to work 8:00 – 5:00, grab a sandwich, go to my class/workout, and not get home until 11:00 p.m. or later. Just as disheartening were the negative comments and jokes some of my friends directed towards me. Guys especially can be brutal with each other. Whenever we got together, a few of my friends enjoyed mimicking karate punches and kicks and saying anything they thought would get under my skin.

All of these things combined made me question whether I was willing to pay the price required of me. I thought about the days when I finished working, physically and mentally exhausted, and simply wanted to go home, grab a cold drink and simply relax. I also considered the dates, parties and social events with my friends I would have to give up. Achieving my goals in Karate would demand much sacrifice on my part.

Thankfully, I had instructors who believed in me and encouraged me through the years. I earned a black belt. And, later I had the privilege to train under a renowned sparring (Kumite) champion.

Many others have dealt with great difficulties in order to achieve their dreams. The type of circumstances I faced can apply in similar ways to you as you set out to reach a goal that will require time, effort, and sacrifice. Hopefully, you can benefit from some of the things I share.

It may be that you are filled with apprehension as you enter a new arena. Perhaps, it is the new boss or teacher that concerns you. Maybe you are questioning if you can measure up to the new challenge. This could be a time when you lack confidence in yourself. Perhaps, even your friends don't support you. Or worse, say things to discourage you. It may seem that your goal is too distant to reach. Don't despair. Remember, you are not alone.

A theme that runs throughout this book is that things always work out much better when you ask God to help you. On the other hand, your struggle will likely be much greater when you don't. Including God, having the assurance that He is with you will turn your anxiety to peace. Along with it, your confidence to deal with your challenge will also increase. Please keep in mind this powerful scripture. "I have the strength for everything through him who empowers me." *(Philippians 4:13 NAB)* You can do anything with Christ by your side.

LESSONS FROM
BUSINESS

Chapter 4

LESSONS FROM BUSINESS

Many of us have dreams about what we want to do when we grow up. From the age of four, my dream was to play baseball in the major leagues. I was on the verge of having that opportunity when a broken leg ended my career during my senior year in college. As a result, my life took an unplanned turn. After graduating, instead of playing baseball, I went into business with my father (and later, my brother.)

In this chapter I share three experiences and the valuable lessons I learned during that time.

My father and I began by acquiring a struggling retail automotive paint store in

West Palm Beach, FL. As this store grew and prospered, it enabled us to purchase two struggling paint factories in Tampa, FL and Miami, FL that manufactured specialized automotive, aircraft, marine and industrial coatings. Along with this purchase we became members (we were grandfathered in) of an exclusive trade association. Only two representatives from any company, (regardless of size) could attend the spring or fall meetings held in the finest resorts in Florida or West Virginia.

I was in my mid-twenties when I attended my first meeting. I was awestruck and full of apprehension as I met and socialized with the CEOs, senior vice presidents and top executives of the biggest petroleum, solvents and chemical companies in the country. I found myself in a whole different league. I also privately held the opinion that many of them would be snobs.

However, I quickly learned otherwise. The first event my wife and I attended was a reception. We were the newest and youngest couple there. I felt completely out of place. Right away, a highly respected member and his wife came over to welcome us. He made us feel comfortable by joking about how awkward they felt their first meeting. He also reassured me that we had a great association with many nice people, and we were going to fit right in.

A little bit later, another man and I bumped into each other. He asked me if this was my first time there. I said yes. He said, me too. We shared big smiles as we introduced ourselves and our wives to each other. We spent much of that reception talking together. They were friendly, and I found out that they were down to earth, regular people. It turned out that he was a newly elected senator from Louisiana and was at the meeting to give a talk concerning government regulations affecting our industry.

As I look back, I find it interesting that something like a reception could serve as a teacher to see that people are people regardless of position.

There is one more experience regarding this organization I want to share. Years later, ten of us were having dinner together. One of the men commented that the focus was usually on the men or our jobs. We shifted all the focus to the women. One by one they shared about their education, family, hobbies and anything else they wanted to say. The last woman to share was the wife of a top executive from a large company. As she began to speak, her lips began to quiver and tears began to roll down her face. All the women rushed to comfort her, and the men did their best to be supportive. Finally, she was able to say she had met her husband when she waited on him at a restaurant. And, even after many years of marriage to this successful man, she still worked at the restaurant because the people there were like family to her. She confided she was apprehensive about what others would think. Rather than holding back she had courageously decided to share something that was difficult for her. It was an emotional moment that deepened our friendship that night.

Let me share a few observations from some of the things I have mentioned. If my baseball career had not ended abruptly, I probably would never have developed successful companies with my father and my brother. In retrospect, I value that much more than anything I could have accomplished on my own. In the same way, God can redirect even bad things that happen to you and turn them for your good if you place your trust in Him.

Do not make the same mistake I made by pre-judging or assuming something negative about other people before you get to know them. Wherever you go, whatever you do, whoever you meet, take the time to get to know someone before you form an opinion about them. "Stop judging by appearances, but judge justly." *(John 7:24*

NAB) Many times the assumptions you make stem from your own insecurities trying to take the upper hand in your life.

One last thing, please remember that God is moved when you are willing to make yourself vulnerable and practice humility. "When he is dealing with the arrogant, he is stern, but to the humble he shows kindness." *(Proverbs 3:34 NAB)* Living a life of humility runs contrary to our nature. It is not easy. However, the rewards are priceless.

Two Choices, One Decision

In business as in life, there are often ups and downs. There was a difficult period at one our companies that created a great deal of stress for my father and me. It happened late in my business career, at a time after I had decided to sincerely follow God and really sought His will.

There was a time when we were faced with a complex situation and we had an important decision to make. However, there were two distinct options that would take us in very different directions. For weeks I prayed seeking counsel from God. Even after much prayer and seeking the Lord, I did not receive an answer or any clear-cut leading. The day came when a definitive decision needed to be made. We still did not know what was the right thing to do. Frustrated and confused we went for a walk just prior to going to the final, crucial meeting with our attorneys. As we walked and talked, I prayed silently. Thankfully during that walk, God's still, small voice spoke to my thoughts "Do not worry, because you have sought me and placed this problem in my hands, I will bless whatever decision you make. Whether you go to the left or to the right, everything will turn out well." I felt a great peace come over me and knew at that moment that God had just answered my prayers. Everything did work out in a positive way.

There are a few things to be gleaned from this experience. I don't want you to think that your prayers will be answered in the same way every time. There are times when it seems God takes a long time to answer. You may question whether He even heard you to begin with. The time between your prayer and the answer can prove to be a difficult test of faith.

But, even when He waits to the last moment, He will be faithful to answer you. "The Lord has heard my plea; the Lord has accepted my prayer." *(Psalm 6:10 NAB)*

Rest assured, every single one of your prayers is heard. And, every single one of your prayers will be answered.

The Last Sale

There came a time when our family decided to sell our companies. After thirteen years in the paint and solvent business, my father and I became sensitized to the chemicals. Exposure to them would trigger headaches and allergic reactions. As a result, we stayed away from our offices at the factories. This made it impossible for us to maintain the personal, hands-on approach to which we were accustomed. In addition, my brother was overseeing the management of our retail stores, and we were not able to provide him the support we had in the past.

In steps, we began selling our factories and stores. Eventually, we were left with a group of four stores. A buyer made us a proposal that would require us to accept the offer, take the necessary inventories and close the deal within a relatively short period of time. We were only lukewarm about the offer. However, it would enable us to achieve our goals.

At this point, there is something I want to interject. In the preceding several years, I had made the decision to follow Jesus. Recently, my father had made the same decision. Now we found ourselves on the verge of selling our last business. This time, we took time to pray in order to seek God's guidance and help.

Unexpectedly, another buyer came forward who was interested in talking to us. The problem was that we had a fast approaching deadline to close on the existing offer. It was always our practice to carefully analyze a deal, then determine who and how we would make our presentation. The night before the important meeting with the new prospective buyer, I started going over the details with my father. He cut me off and said that he was not going to even think about it. This time, we were going to say a prayer and leave everything in God's hands. The next day, without a plan or strategy, my father outlined terms that included: **(1)** a higher price; **(2)** acceptance of the inventory based on **our** estimated value. (A physical inventory would not be possible due to the time constraints of the first offer). Incredibly, the new buyer agreed. We sold our last business without taking a physical inventory, and we received a higher price than the initial offer. Both parties got what they needed, and the sale turned out well for everyone. As we drove

42

home, my father said to me, "only God could have worked out all the details of this sale." I said to him, "Dad, can you imagine how much better things would have been if we had done this from the beginning?"

In this case, we came to the very end of our business journey before we realized we could have taken a much better path. There were some regrets because many things could have been done much differently over the years.

What if…that is a question I could ask many times over. What if I had prayed through all my decisions? What if I had sought God's help for all my problems? What if I had always trusted Him with my life? I hope you benefit from my mistakes. You can change the 'what if'…. In your life into a positive confession. I choose to trust.

I choose to pray. I choose to love. I choose to believe. I hope you choose to seek God in all things.

LEARNING FROM
OTHERS

Chapter 5

LEARNING FROM OTHERS

Aside from our family members, our friends, and the people we encounter can play significant roles in our lives. Listening to others, observing them and learning from their example will undoubtedly influence the way we think and act. Some of them will teach us valuable lessons, while at the same time, be a blessing to us. I hope you will benefit from the blessings and lessons I received from one such friend.

Adrienne

At the time I met Adrienne, she was the director of a major community organization in Tampa, Fl. She was full of energy, had a big smile for everyone, and a wonderful personality to match. Her accomplishments were many, and she was well liked and respected wherever she went. As our friendship grew, I learned she was compassionate, loving and embraced a deep faith in God. It became our custom once every several months to meet at a park in Tampa, take long walks, pray together and then go out for lunch.

One day as we walked, she told me she felt God was leading her to resign her position and adopt three minority children who had been born with AIDS. She confided she was apprehensive for many reasons. How would she manage financially? What would it take to care for and raise three children? Especially since she had no experience. Lastly, she was conflicted about giving up a job she loved. One that identified her and gave her acceptance in the community. However, it was most important for her to follow her convictions.

Many changes took place in her life when she transitioned from her job to raising children with special needs. For one thing, people would often stare when they went to restaurants and other places because they were a different skin color. Other minority adults resented her adopting the children and made racial slurs as well as making things difficult for her. She found that many of the people who were friendly with her when she had her high profile job no longer called, socialized or included her in their plans. Two of the children adored her. One was rebellious and acted out with negative behavior.

There were moments of sadness and heartbreak. Such as when she had to deal with the prejudice of misguided adults. Or when her rebellious son's behavior led him into trouble with the authorities. But, there were also times of great joy and fulfillment. Most notably, the many special times when her other children expressed how much they loved her. There was a struggle back and forth in her life. Nevertheless, she always maintained her faith in God. Through it all, she exhibited grace, dignity and love. Her example helped me understand the meaning of going the distance with God.

The Apostle Paul expressed it perfectly with his words, "I have competed well; I have finished the race; I have kept the faith." (*2 Timothy 4:7 NAB*)

I once heard someone say, "If you can't see Jesus in the person next to you, you will not be able to see Jesus at all." Whether we realize it or not, we are surrounded by people who personify Jesus. However, it is up to us to open our eyes in order to see Him and open our hearts to receive Him.

My friend offers us a glimpse of Jesus through her experiences. Following your convictions may come at a cost. Perhaps, it will mean giving up something you value or enjoy. The road may prove to be quite bumpy along the way. Other people may ridicule, scorn and insult you. Be prepared, if it happened to Jesus, it could happen to you. The people you are making a sacrifice for may appreciate it. On the other hand, they may not. Be prepared for that too. Some friends may exit your life when you are no longer useful to them. But, the loyalty and love of true friends through thick and thin will sustain you. Most importantly, trusting Christ will give you the strength to finish the race and keep the faith.

Spiritual MD

When I was thirty-three years old, I was diagnosed with a malignancy in my left leg that required major surgery. During that time I received a lesson I have never forgotten.

The day before the surgery, I was admitted to Shands Hospital in Gainesville, FL. I was quite anxious because I had signed a consent form to amputate my left leg if the surgeon decided it was necessary. A friend of mine (who happened to be a doctor) called me in the afternoon and offered to come visit me. He did not arrive until after 10:00 p.m., following a long, grueling day of consults and surgeries.

When he came into the room, he said several things that made a profound impression on me. He informed me that when he arrived at my room, he did not know what to say to me. So, before going in he stopped outside the door and prayed to God to give him wisdom and to speak through him. He also told me that the next morning, when I was taken to the operating room, I would not have anything with me. I would only be covered by a hospital gown. He counseled me that before I was given the anesthesia, to say this silently, "Lord, I offer you myself and this surgery to you. That is all I have to give you today."

I followed his advice the next day. The surgery went well, my leg was fine, and I never had a recurrence of cancer. But, I never forgot his example. Over the years, there have been times when it was inconvenient, or I simply felt too tired to help someone else. Recollecting my friend's late night visit after a long day pushes me to do for others what he did for me. Up until that night I had never seen anyone stop, take the time to pray, and ask God to provide them with the right thoughts and words. It is now my practice to do this before I try to help anyone else. Perhaps, this will encourage you to do the same. One last insight, there may be times when you feel completely empty with nothing to give to God. Not so. Even if you have nothing, you can offer yourself. Wherever you are, whatever the circumstance, the Lord is only a whisper away, and He will accept you just as you are.

A Great Role Model

I was blessed. I had a role model who taught me many valuable life lessons. He wasn't the biggest, or the fastest or the strongest. But, he was a great man. Hopefully, some of the things I learned from him will help you, too.

During World War II, my father was stationed in Cuba. After the war, he stayed and taught at the University of Santo Tomas De Villanueva in Havana. When I was born, he went into the paint business. At that time, the majority of petroleum based solvents were imported as finished products into the country. My father negotiated exclusive deals with some of the oil companies to manufacture some of those products in the country. He invested all he had in a factory and warehousing. It would have been a hugely successful and profitable business. That is, until Fidel Castro took power in Cuba and confiscated American-owned companies. Literally overnight, my father and my family lost everything.

We were lucky to be able to leave Cuba and move to Florida. My family arrived with less than one thousand dollars to start all over again. My father did some tutoring and sales work to provide for us and save money. After a number of years, he entered into a business relationship with someone he did not know very well. They had been negotiating an agreement with a company when one day he learned that this person and the company had made their own dcal. My father lost his business a second time. Please hold that thought as I move into another area.

I have previously mentioned that my father and I went into business together after I graduated from college. My brother joined us when he graduated. Together, we were able to build our companies, which we ultimately sold. All this happened within a span of fifteen years. After which, my father retired, and I rededicated my time and energy into charitable and ministry related work.

One day, after one of my overseas trips, he and I had a long conversation during which he asked me many questions about the trip. He listened intently as I shared about many of the things that had taken place. He was genuinely interested, and then said something I did not expect to hear, "Son, I am very happy for you and I wish I had what you have right now." I answered, "Dad, what I have is Jesus, and you can have Him in the same way right now if you want." Right then and there he humbly said a Sinner's Prayer and invited Jesus into his life in a brand new way. He was almost seventy years old. It was one of the most important moments in both our lives.

There is one more thing regarding my father that I want to share. Even in retirement, my father was active. Because of his experience, calm personality and analytical mind, he served on the Board of Trustees at two prestigious universities in Connecticut and Florida. In Tampa, he was on the Board of a hospital and a school for underprivileged children. He was also on the board of an ecological company in Stuart, FL.

Although he was calm in the way he dealt with things, health-related issues had always created great anxiety for him. In time, he developed digestive problems. Every meal was followed by a great deal of pain. Finally, he was admitted into the hospital for a full work-up and evaluation. As he was undergoing all the medical tests, I expected to see the anxiety I had seen in the past. To my surprise, I did not. Ultimately, he was diagnosed with terminal liver cancer. His doctors privately called to tell me the difficult news.

When I arrived at his room in the hospital, he asked me to close the door because there was something he wanted to tell me. This is what he said, "Son, I have prayed and I feel I have done everything the Lord has asked me to do. And, I don't feel

he is asking me to do anything else. I am
fine with that and I am at peace." And, he
was. His countenance and demeanor
exhibited peace and a supernatural grace I
had never witnessed in him before. At that
moment, he embodied the following
scripture, "Have no anxiety at all, but in
everything, by prayer and petition, with
thanksgiving, make your requests known to
God. Then the peace of God that surpasses
all understanding will guard your hearts and
minds in Christ Jesus." (*Philippians 4:6-7
NAB)* To the very end of his life, he taught
me.

Let's examine the experiences I
mentioned under a spiritual light. (**1**) Even
when you face defeat and all appears lost,
you are called to hold on, to trust, to move
forward and to persevere. The Lord can

help you overcome any setback you face in life. **(2)** The wisest thing you can do is to be united with God. Regardless of your wealth, education, talent, position or power submitting to Him in humility is the best thing you can do. By the way, there is no age restriction. **(3)** Giving yourself to Jesus will change your life. As you obey His commands, your old nature of anger, worry, fear and anxiety will be transformed into one of love with all its characteristics *(1Corinthians 13:4-7).* When all is said and done, His supernatural peace will fill your life.

LET GOD BE IN
CONTROL

Chapter 6

LET GOD BE IN CONTROL

Most of us inwardly know that we are not as strong or as smart as we would like for other people to think we are. Deep down we know there is only one person who is all-knowing, all-seeing, and infallible. And, even though He invites us to turn to Him so that He can help us, we often put up a struggle. It's our nature to want to do things our way. WE want to be in control, and we don't like to let it go.

Yet, that is what we must do in order to receive God's best for us. Regardless of the circumstances, submitting to God's will is the first step we need to take before He can take control over the situation and work things out for us.

For a moment, imagine that you are a student taking flying lessons. You begin in the classroom and eventually get airborne. At every stage you instructor is in control. In the air, he holds the controls as he instructs you. He knows everything you don't. It is his goal to teach you to enjoy flying in a safe manner.

In a similar way, imagine that throughout your life, you are a student pilot, and God is your instructor. If you can acknowledge that God knows infinitely more than you, then it stands to reason you would be wise to let Him help you by turning the controls over to Him as he teaches and guides you.

A Difficult Prayer

There are times when submitting to God's will can be painful, even sad. Some years ago I had a dear friend. She embodied all the qualities that would describe a true friend. She was thoughtful, compassionate, understanding, loving, loyal, and if those things were not enough, she also had a great sense of humor, wonderful personality and lived life to the fullest. Did I mention she was an incredible cook? She had it all. Let me not neglect to say that she also possessed a deep, abiding, childlike faith in God.

Friendships grow and get stronger as friends share in each other's joys and trials, ups and downs, the good times and the tough times. That certainly was the case with my friend. Somehow, went through a lot of things together. But, there came a time when her trust in God and mine also was put to the test.

My friend had to undergo an operation. The robotic surgery that was performed went terribly wrong. The lining of her colon was perforated, and sepsis followed. Only a second emergency surgery saved her life. However, she was never the same again.

In the succeeding months, the incision would not heal properly. Over time, she developed multiple infections. Her doctor was perplexed. She was finally referred to an oncologist who diagnosed her with stage IV cancer. I visited and prayed with her on a regular basis. All the while, her condition continued to deteriorate. Ultimately, she reached a point where she was in a great deal of pain and discomfort. This in turn took its toll on her energy and mental outlook. The steady decline continued over many months.

One afternoon I received a call that things had taken a turn for the worse, and I needed to see her as soon as possible. As I drove to see her, I sought the Lord in prayer, asking Him what should I say to my friend, and how should I pray for her. Almost immediately the answer came in the form of a thought, "pray for whatever she asks."

When I saw her she asked that I pray for her to be released from her pain and for a peaceful death. At that moment, I knew I was going to lose my friend soon. With sadness in my heart, I prayed as she asked. Her request was granted not long afterward.

On the one hand, I am happy for her. Because, she is in Heaven with the Lord.

There is no more pain. No more tears. No more sorrow. On the other hand, I feel her loss and the sadness that accompanies it.

There are several fundamental points I want to present to you regarding my friend's story:

(1) It is important to remember that God is all-knowing and all-seeing. He knows what we don't know. And, sees what we cannot see. He understands every hidden detail regarding each person's life. He understands everything.

(2) We only catch glimpses in most cases. We form opinions and develop desires based on what we know. Quite often, our limited understanding will put our opinions and desires at odds with what God is telling us. Invariably, all of us face decisions when what we want may not line up exactly with what God is revealing to us.

(3) I offer you the advice I have given myself. Release your grip. Give up the control over what you want, and let God work things out His way.

PRAYERS OF
RELEASE

Chapter 7

PRAYERS OF RELEASE

Prayer demands that we release control of what we are praying about to God. By doing so, we release to God the freedom He needs to answer us. I mentioned in a previous book that when we pray, we acknowledge that God is able to do for us what we are not able to do for ourselves. I illustrate this point by sharing several situations I prayed about.

A Nagging Question

Shortly after I made the decision to put God first in all things, I found myself struggling with a question as I prayed. What if God asked me to sell everything I owned and go to work in some remote country? Would I do it?

You see, at the time I had just purchased a home I really liked, most things were going well, and my life was comfortable. For weeks I questioned if I could let go of my security if God told me to. I wrestled in prayer with this question until one day the Holy Spirit helped me with the answer. Finally, that day my prayer went like this, "Lord, I don't want to sell my home, get rid of things I own and uproot my family to some unfamiliar place. But I really do want to put you first. If that is what you tell me, change my heart, make me willing to obey you and cause me to do what you say." For me, this struggle became a step that helped me submit more fully to God.

My Doctors and Me

Another situation I faced involved a time after I had suffered a brainstem hemorrhage. My doctor at the University of Florida arranged a consult with one of the top neurosurgeons in the U.S. in order to review all my records and discuss the options.

We spent one and a half hours going over my medical history. When we finished, the conclusion was that I was not a good candidate for the latest procedures and technology they explored. They also explained that surgery was not a realistic option either. The final option was to do nothing.

As we walked out of the building, my doctor put his arm around my shoulder and asked, "Frank, are you all right?" I said yes as I said goodbye to him. I then continued walking and praying as I processed all the information. This is the conversation I had with God at that moment. "Lord, I came seeking direction as to what to do. All the options were eliminated. You are the only option left. You told me over and over again to put my life in Your hands and to trust You. You have me where you want me. You are the best option. My life is in Your hands." This is the answer I received. "Frank, your life is in my hands. Let me take care of you."

JESUS: ROLE MODEL

Chapter 8

JESUS: ROLE MODEL

It crossed my mind how special it would be if Jesus was teaching a course on Christianity at one of our universities today. Although that is not the case, we still have the ability to hear and learn from Him.

Fortunately, we have His own words written in the Bible. Along with His words, we have a record of events in His life and ministry. These things provide us the information we need to understand and apply His teachings in our lives.

Perhaps Jesus is not teaching a class at a university. But, He continues to reach out to us. In this chapter, we will examine seven important principles He taught us by His words and example. As we focus our spotlight on the perfect model, let's see what He shows us, and let's hear what He has to say.

Humility

"Take my yoke upon you and learn from me, for I am meek and humble of heart; and you will find rest for yourselves." *(Matthew 11:29 NAB)*

Please remember these are the words of Jesus speaking to you and me right now. They deliver a straightforward message. Jesus approaches us in humility. With meekness and a humble heart, He invites us to follow Him and put His teachings into practice in our lives. If we do this, He promises we will find rest for ourselves.

Jesus continues to teach us by describing the quality of humility and the effect it has on us. "The greatest among you must be your servant. Whoever exalts himself will be humbled; but whoever humbles himself will be exalted." (*Matthew 23:11-12 NAB*)

Humility demands that we develop a heart of service for others. It is easy to fall into the trap of basking in the glory and adulation of success. Jesus tells us that whatever success we attain needs to be harnessed and used in the service of others. He reminds us that living humbly will be pleasing to God. On the other hand, prideful, arrogant behavior will not please God.

We are asked to develop an attitude of humility to serve as a foundation in our treatment of others. Again, Jesus gave us a perfect example when He washed the feet of His apostles.

"So when he had washed their feet [and] put his garments back on and reclined at table again, he said to them, "Do you realize what I have done for you? You call me 'teacher' and 'master' and rightly so, for indeed I am. If I, therefore, the master and teacher, have washed your feet, you ought to wash one another's feet. I have given you a model to follow, so that as I have done for you, you should also do." *(John 13:12-15 NAB)*

Jesus also taught about humility by holding up a little child as an example. "Whoever humbles himself like this child is the greatest in the kingdom of heaven." *(Matthew 18:4 NAB)* Set aside your knowledge, position and power. Come with the heart of a little child. Trusting.

Innocent. How profound, we can develop humility by imitating humble children.

Please keep this in mind, we develop humility. It does not fall into our lives like ripened fruit falling from a tree. It takes effort. It does not necessarily happen all at once. It takes time. As our thinking and attitude change, the way we act will also change. Jesus does not ask us to do something that is not possible. On the contrary, all things are possible with Him. Whether or not we are humble is our choice.

Compassion

"And a leper came to Jesus, beseeching Him and falling on his knees before Him, and saying, "If You are willing, You can make me clean." Moved with compassion, Jesus stretched out His hand and touched him, and said to him "I am willing, be cleansed." Immediately the leprosy left him and he was cleansed."
(Mark 1:40-42 NASB)

For a moment, switch places with Jesus. Imagine that someone with an incurable disease, someone who is desperate for a cure comes to you begging to be healed. If you have the ability to heal this person, what would you do? Would you see the suffering, feel the pain and touch the hopelessness like Jesus did? Would you place your hand on the visible wound if

there is one? Would you understand this
person's desperation? Would you tell him
(her) of course, I will help you, be healed?
This scripture from the Gospel of Mark
perfectly describes compassion. Jesus
personified it for us.

By His example, Jesus taught us to be
aware of the needs of the people we
encounter in our lives. Not only that, but to
do something about it if we have the ability.

For example, as He traveled, He came
across many people. The lame, crippled,
blind and sick would be easy to see.
However, Jesus was well aware of the
condition of others as well. Two scriptures
illustrate this for us:

"In those days, when there was again
a large crowd and they had nothing to eat,

Jesus called His disciples and said to them, "I feel compassion for the people because they have remained with Me now three days and have nothing to eat. If I send them away hungry to their homes, they will faint on the way; and some of them have come from a great distance." (*Mark 8:1-3 NASB*)

"Seeing the people, He felt compassion for them, because they were distressed and dispirited like sheep without a shepherd." *(Matthew 9:36 NASB)*

Every need He encountered was important to Him. Whether it was pain, suffering, despair or hunger, it mattered enough for Him to do something about it.

As we look at Jesus, we should be inspired to look around us. To become more perceptive and sensitive of those around us.

And, to see what we can do to make a difference in someone else's life. Compassion takes us beyond sympathy and empathy, it demands us to take action.

Prayer

"In the days when he was in the flesh, he offered prayers and supplications with loud cries and tears to the one who was able to save him from death, and he was heard because of his reverence." *(Hebrews 5:7 NAB)*

When all is said and done, the essence of prayer is an acknowledgement of our reliance and dependency on God. Jesus taught us that submitting to the Father's will is a vital foundation of prayer. There is only one God who is all knowing, all seeing, and all powerful. And, it is up to you and me to acknowledge Him and submit to Him. This can be difficult because doing so forces us to let go of all control. Yet, even when we don't understand, Jesus showed us that is what we must do. In the Garden of

Gethsemane, "He advanced a little and fell prostrate in prayer, saying, "My Father, if it is possible, let this cup pass from me; yet, not as I will, but as you will." *(Matthew 26:39 NAB)*

This prayer spoken during the agony in the garden illustrates for us the need to submit to the Father's will.

The gospels contain many instances of Jesus getting away to be alone to pray (Matthew 14:23, Mark 1:35, Mark 6:46, Luke 5:16, Luke 6:12). He showed that it is essential for us to pray at all times.

"Rising very early before dawn, he left and went off to a deserted place, where he prayed." *(Mark 1:35 NAB)*

I want to point out that we need to approach prayer with the same determination and persistence Jesus did.

The Father does not have a secretary making appointments for you and me to have a conversation with Him. Like Jesus, we can approach Him any time. "In those days he departed to the mountain to pray, and he spent the night in prayer to God." *(Luke 6:12 NAB)* Notice, one time Jesus rose early before dawn to pray. Another time, He spent the night in prayer. We are invited to follow his example.

As we do this, we need to pay attention to His instructions. A fundamental command is for us to pray to the Father. The prayer He taught His followers begins "Our Father in Heaven" *(Matthew 6:9-13)*. He also told us that after He returned to the

Father, we are to ask the Father directly using His name *(John 16:23, 16:26-27)*.

Prayer is an act of faith. It places our trust in God to do what we can't ourselves. And, have the confidence that He will meet our needs when we pray in accordance with His will.

"Ask and it will be given to you; seek and you will find; knock and the door will be opened to you. For everyone who asks, receives; and the one who seeks, finds; and to the one who knocks, the door will be opened. Which one of you would hand his son a stone when he asks for a loaf of bread, or a snake when he asks for a fish? If you then, who are wicked, know how to give good gifts to your children, how much more will your heavenly Father give good things to those who ask him." *(Matthew 7:7-11 NAB)*

As we look to Jesus for direction, there is one basic thing we must do if we want our prayers to be effective. Obey. Simply follow His example and do what He says.

Obedience

But Samuel said: Does the Lord so delight in holocausts and sacrifices as in obedience to the command of the Lord? Obedience is better than sacrifice, and submission than the fat of rams." *(1 Samuel 15:22 NAB)*

Obedience can be difficult to achieve. It is our nature to want to do things our way. It often becomes a struggle when we find ourselves having to obey someone else. All of us need help in this area. For that reason, Jesus is the perfect model to look at.

Just think, He had supernatural abilities, and the resources of the entire universe were at His disposal. Yet, He humbly came in human form and obeyed the will of the Father in all things, even death on a cross. Although our obedience can never accomplish what Jesus did for mankind, we are nevertheless called to obey the will of the Father just like Him. As the scripture says: obedience is better than sacrifice.

In addition, obedience to God's will enables us to receive the contents of this promise from Jesus. "Whoever has my commandments and observes them is the one who loves me. And whoever loves me will be loved by my Father, and I will love him and reveal myself to him." *(John 14:21 NAB)*

I believe that all of us understand that we can't always have things our way. Whether we like it or not, we have to obey laws, rules and regulations. We also need to obey people who are in positions of authority over us. That includes obedience to our parents. Although, how many of us can say we have done that without putting up an argument? Obedience to God's will is often easier said than done. The choice is ours. It is a decision each one of us must make individually.

Forgiveness

"But Jesus was saying, "Father, forgive them; for they do not know what they are doing." And they cast lots, dividing up His garments among themselves." *(Luke 23:34 NASB)*

In just these few words Jesus conveys a powerful message of forgiveness. Can you imagine how He felt after being set up, ridiculed, scorned, stripped, beaten and crucified? In spite of this miscarriage of justice, Jesus interceded on behalf of the people who had done these things to Him. To the very end of His life, He practiced what He preached. "But I say to you, love your enemies, and pray for those who persecute you." *(Matthew 5:44 NAB)*

His words and His example on forgiveness provide a cornerstone of His gospel. It is really a simple message. If you want to be forgiven when you do something wrong, first forgive anyone who has wronged you. *(Mark 11:25, Matthew 6:12)*

I believe most of us get it. We understand what we should do. Yet, forgiving some people can prove to be extremely difficult. Everyone is not the same. It seems there is always someone who is more obnoxious, more arrogant and easier to despise than others. However, the message of forgiveness is not complicated. Find a way to look beyond someone else's faults, overcome the need to get even in any way, and, no matter what was said or done against you, determine to wish that person well.

Undoubtedly, this is a struggle for all of us. At one time, the Apostle Peter wrestled with this issue *(Matthew 18:21-22, Luke 17:4)*

"Then Peter approaching asked Him, 'Lord, if my brother sins against me, how often must I forgive him? As many as seven times?' Jesus answered, "I say to you, not seven times but seventy-seven times." *(Matthew 18-21-22 NAB)*

All of us have free will. We can choose to forgive others and be in a place to receive God's best, or we can choose not to and deprive ourselves of His best for us. It is our choice.

Giving

"John answered and said, "No one can receive anything except what has been given him from Heaven." *(John 3:27 NAB)*

The greatest gift mankind received from Heaven is Jesus. Not only did He give Himself for us, He also taught us how to give of ourselves. With very clear words, He instructed us "For I was hungry, and you gave Me something to eat; I was thirsty, and you gave Me something to drink; I was a stranger, and you invited Me in; naked, and you clothed Me; I was sick, and you visited Me; I was in prison, and you came to Me." *(Matthew 25:35-36 NASB)*

Throughout His ministry, Jesus gave of Himself. Every act of kindness, love, healing, mercy and compassion set the standard for all of us to follow. He taught us and He showed us what to do. Everything we freely received from Him we are to freely give away to others. *(Matthew 10:8)*

Jesus also had something to say about financial giving. Besides giving of our time and talent, we are also called to give of our treasure. This, too, is an important way we show our love for God and put Him first. We should do this willingly and cheerfully. "Give, and it will be given to you. They will pour into your lap a good measure – pressed down, shaken together, and running over. For by your standard of measure it will be measured to you in return." *(Luke 6:38 NASB)*

Another valuable lesson on giving can be found in the Gospel of Matthew. "But when you give to the poor, do not let your left hand know what your right hand is doing, so that your giving will be in secret; and your Father who sees what is done in secret will reward you." *(Matthew 6:3-4 NASB)* Why we give, how we give, and what we give will be noted by God, and He will reward our obedience and sacrifice.

On one occasion, Jesus was at the temple where He observed the rich putting in their gifts into the collection box and then a poor widow came and put in two small copper coins *(Luke 21:1-4)*. He used this story to illustrate that even a large contribution given out of someone's surplus is not as valuable in God's sight as two small coins given out of poverty. Look at it this way, a small gift given sacrificially is more pleasing to God than large leftovers.

Each one of us has different gifts and talents (artistic, physical, intellectual, financial). Whatever ability we have is to be used for more than just our own benefit. It should also be used for the benefit of others. If we do this, we will please God.

Love

"For God so loved the world, that He gave His only begotten Son, that whoever believes in Him shall not perish, but have eternal life." *(John 3:16 NASB)*

Our Father in Heaven, the origin of love, gave His only Son, Jesus, to reconcile us to Himself. Can any of us grasp such a sacrifice? This is not even a remotely adequate illustration. But, can you imagine a world leader say, the President of Russia, laying down his life for a peasant in Siberia? In contrast, God's love for us cannot be measured.

It would take an entire book or series of books to properly discuss the subject of love. At this point, we are only going to focus on several things Jesus told us. He said, "Greater love has no one than this, that one lay down his life for his friends." *(John 15:13 NASB)*

Jesus paid the ultimate price to wipe out our debt. Now, we may not be required to physically die for others. However, we can lay down our life for others when we sacrifice of ourselves to help them. So, how does that look? Would you be willing to take the money you saved for a candlelight dinner in order to buy groceries for that family in need you met this afternoon? Would you forego the party you looked forward to in order to visit a sick friend?

Jesus also taught that the greatest and second greatest commandments demand the same thing.

"He said to him, "You shall love the Lord, your God, with all your heart, with all your soul, and with all your mind. This is the greatest and the first commandment. The second is like it: You shall love your neighbor as yourself." *(Matthew 22:37-39 NAB)*

Jesus gave the apostle Paul His gospel by revelation *(Galatians 1:11-12)*. He, in turn, wrote much of the New Testament. If we listen closely, I believe we can hear Jesus instructing us through Paul's words. In the first letter to the Corinthians *(1 Corinthians 13:1-8),* we are told that possessing great gifts without love is worthless. Likewise, performing extraordinary deeds with no love is meaningless.

God is love. Love is at the core of everything Jesus said and did. The depth of His love is beyond our ability to comprehend.

"For I am convinced that neither death, nor life, nor angels, nor principalities, nor present things, nor future things, nor powers, nor height, nor depth, nor any other creature will be able to separate us from the love of God in Christ Jesus our Lord. *(Romans 8:38-39 NAB)*

CONCLUDING
THOUGHTS

Chapter 9

CONCLUDING THOUGHTS

As we come to the end of this book, there are a few final thoughts I want to share with you. It is my hope that you have related to the things I wrote about; and hopefully, my comments have been helpful. As you can see, I did not write about any great accomplishments in my life. The reason is because I did not invent anything, did not find the cure for any disease or achieve anything anyone would consider extraordinary. As a matter of fact, some of the experiences I shared can be described as insignificant in many ways. Yet, even insignificant experiences can serve as vehicles to teach us and mold us. It is my guess that many of you reading this fall into the same category as I do.

A thought that has crossed my mind from time to time is this, "I wish I knew then what I know now." I am sure most of us wish we could change some of the things we did in our past. And, one of the best ways to learn from our mistakes is by taking time to examine ourselves honestly. I encourage you to "take a step back," "take a deep breath," and reflect on your life. Let me suggest you do this with a positive attitude. Guard yourself against the negativism that may try to enter when you acknowledge your past and present shortcomings and failings.

There are many self-help books on the market. This is not one of them. However,

I do have a final piece of advice. Whoever you are, wherever you are, whatever your situation, take the time to examine yourself in light of God's will for you. The bottom line is simply this, does God exist or doesn't He? Is Jesus alive or not? Is your faith real or is it a myth?

There is only one answer to each question. I pray that this book challenges you to look at your life and brings you nearer to God.

Author Profile

Frank Esposito Jr. was born in Havana, Cuba. He moved to Florida at the age of ten. Later, he attended Palm Beach College and St. Thomas University on baseball scholarships where he graduated with honors. Along with his father and brother, he formed successful companies. At the age of 36 he sold his business and dedicated his life to charitable and ministry-related work. He and his wife, Marilyn, live in Tierra Verde, Florida.